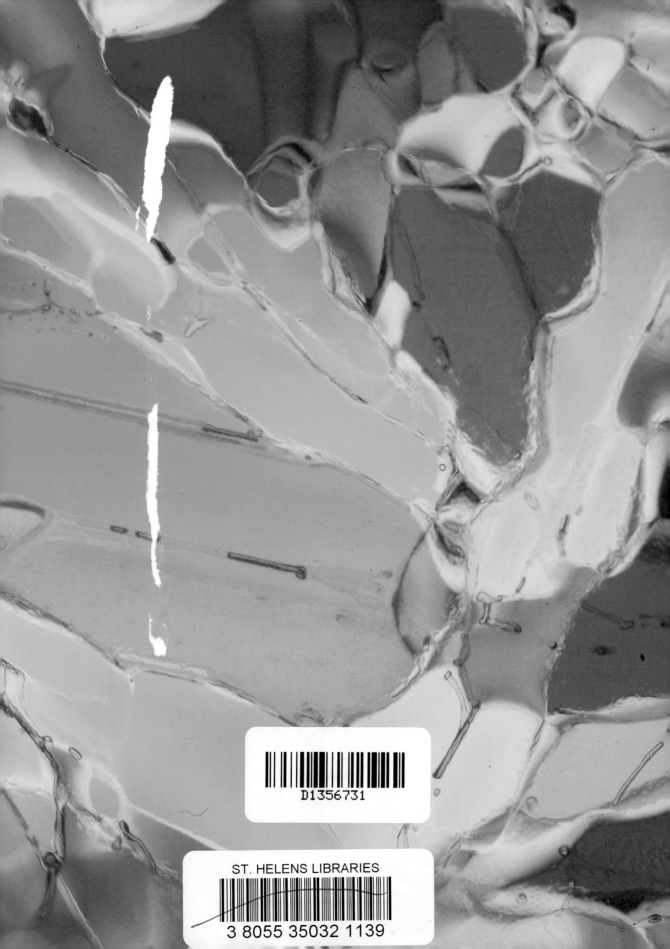

AMAZING MATERIALS

Solids, liquids and gases

Rob Colson

WAYLAND

First published in Great Britain
in 2017 by Wayland
Copyright © Hodder and Stoughton, 2017

Wayland
An imprint of Hachette
Children's Group
Part of Hodder and Stoughton
Carmelite House
50 Victoria Embankment
London EC4Y 0DZ

Executive editor: Adrian Cole
Produced by Tall Tree Ltd
Written by: Rob Colson
Designer: Ben Ruocco

ISBN: 978 1 5263 0500 8
10 9 8 7 6 5 4 3 2 1

An Hachette UK Company
www.hachette.co.uk
www.hachettechildrens.co.uk

Printed and bound in China

The website addresses (URLs) included
in this book were valid at the time of
going to press. However, it is possible
that contents or addresses may have
changed since the publication of this book.
No responsibility for any such changes
can be accepted by either the author or
the Publisher.

MIX
Paper from
responsible sources
FSC® C104740
FSC
www.fsc.org

t-top, b-bottom, l-left, r-right, c-centre
front cover-fc, back cover-bc
All images courtesy of Dreamstime.co
unless indicated:
Inside front Rudolf Vancura; fc,
bc Pablo631; fctc Erickn; fctl, 13cr
Fireflyphoto; fccl Okea; fcc, 15b
Flashdevelop; fcbr, 16b BCritchley; fcb
iStockphoto/J-Palys; bctr Cookelma;
bctl Rickdeacon; bccl Mrosanna; 1cl, 7
Tiero; 4-5 Dedmazay; 5tr Civicol3 Stu
Associato; 6l Morganka; 6c, 7tr, 28bl
Inkoly; 7b shutterstock/Sementer; 8b
Tobkatrina; 8b NOAA; 9bc Lukaves; 1C
Norbert Buchholz; 11tl, 31tr Stockakia
11br, 19t, 26br, 29t Mexrix; 11bl Freks
12b Jgroup; 13tl NASA; 14b Sergieiev;
15t Terra24; 15br Caraman; 16-17
Andreadonetti; 16tr U.S. Marine Corps
16bl Anastasia Sorokina; 17cr Oljensa;
17crb Justinjohnson555; 17br Mimadec
18cl Mcininch; 18cr, 19cl Fotoedgaras;
19tl Shawnhemp; 19tr Charles Haynes
Creative Commons AttributionShareali
19bl Dmstudio; 19br Larisa Vasilyeva;
20b Essentialimagemedia; 21tr NASA;
Jamenpercy; 22bl Blinow61; 22br Dtop
22tr Jörg Beuge; 23tr Vkjr; 23c Lightz
23b Juliarstudio; 24cr McLaren Ltd; 2
25b Amichaelbrown; 24bl Anton/Creat
Commons AttributionSharealike; 25tc
Anton Brand; 25cl Jason7825/Creative
Commons AttributionSharealike; 25cr
Digitalg; 26tl, 30br Sabthai; 26bl Mlp7:
27t Titosart; 28tl Supertrooper; 28tr
Goinyk; 28br Twindesigner; 29c Fedor
Labyntsev; 29bc Jianghongyan; 30c Ja
Kirchner; 32t Stylephotographs

Solid, liquid or gas?

Matter is made of tiny atoms or molecules. It takes the form of a solid, liquid or a gas depending on the way these particles bond with one another.

Solid

The particles in a solid are packed close to one another and held together by **strong bonds**. The particles in a solid can vibrate, but cannot move around. Solids have a fixed shape and cannot easily be compressed (squashed).

Gas

The particles in a gas are far apart and arranged in a **random way**. They are not bonded to one another. The particles in a gas move quickly in all directions, meaning that a gas fills any container holding it. The particles can be forced closer together, meaning that a gas can be compressed.

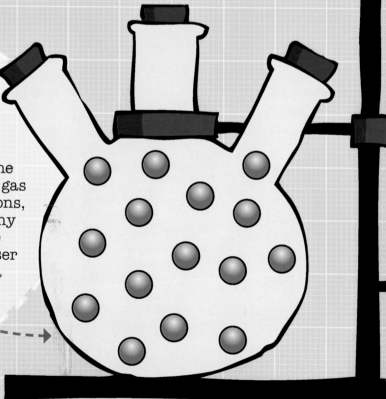

Liquid

The particles in a liquid are close together but arranged in a random way. They are held together **by weak bonds**. The particles in a liquid can move around one another. This means that liquids have no fixed shape, but can flow. Like solids, liquids cannot easily be compressed.

TRY THIS

Take the front wheel of a bicycle and let the air out of the tyre. Now take a bicycle pump and pump air back into the tyre. The tyre is made of a flexible solid rubber. The rubber does not get bigger. Instead, more and more air is squeezed into the tyre. This increases the pressure inside, making the tyre feel hard to the touch.

Hydraulics

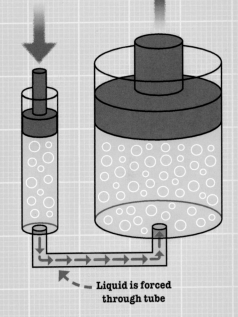

Liquid is forced through tube

Liquids have a fixed volume. Hydraulic systems, such as car lifts, use liquids to **transfer a force** from one part of the machine to another.

Pressure

A gas inside a container exerts a pressure. This is caused by particles **randomly colliding** with the inside of the container. The more gas there is in the container, the greater the pressure.

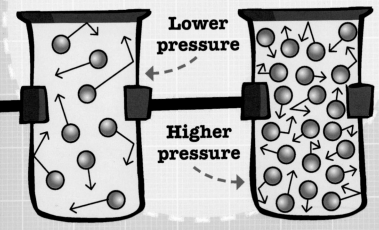

Lower pressure

Higher pressure

Hard
and soft

All solids hold their shape
when no forces are applied
to them, but some solids are
much harder than others.
Their hardness depends on
the way the molecules or
atoms are arranged.

Graphite
molecular
structure

Carbon forms

Graphite and diamond are both made
from carbon atoms, but they have very
different qualities. In graphite, the atoms
are arranged **in layers that slide easily over
one another**. The 'lead' in pencils is actually
graphite. When you press the end of the
pencil against paper, it leaves a trail of
graphite as **the layers rub off**.

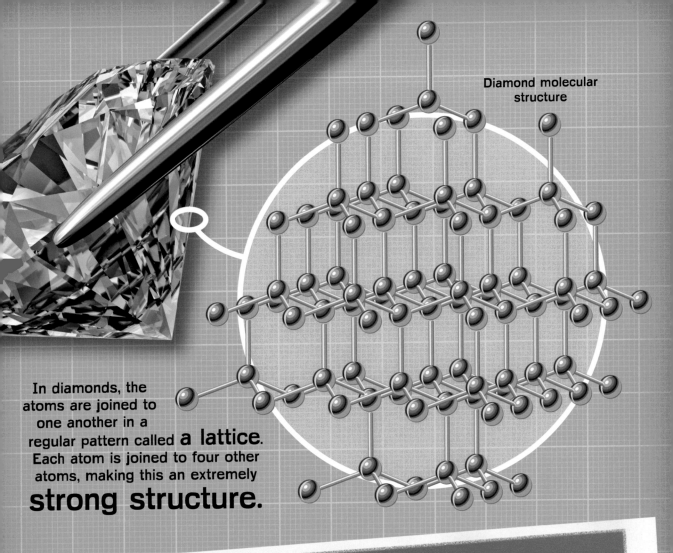

Diamond molecular structure

In diamonds, the atoms are joined to one another in a regular pattern called **a lattice**. Each atom is joined to four other atoms, making this an extremely **strong structure.**

Hardness scale

Mineral rocks are ranked on a hardness scale from 1 to 10, based on how easy it is to **scratch the surface**. This is called the

Mohs scale.

At the bottom is the softest mineral, talc, with a score of 1. Talc is soft enough to scratch with your fingernail. The hardest mineral, diamond, has a score of 10. In reality, diamonds are thought to be **1,600 times harder** than talc.

Increasing hardness

Mineral Name	Scale Number	Common Object
Diamond	10	
Corundum	9	Drill tip (8.5)
Topaz	8	
Quartz	7	Steel nail (6.5)
Orthoclase	6	Knife (5.5)
Apatite	5	
Fluorite	4	Copper coin (3.5)
Calcite	3	Fingernail (2.5)
Gypsum	2	
Talc	1	

Crystals and glass

Solids with a regular molecular structure are called crystalline. The crystals take different shapes depending on how their molecules are arranged. Amorphous solids such as glass have an irregular molecular structure.

Six-sided snowflakes

Snowflakes are **ice crystals**. Each snowflake has a unique shape, but they are all **six-sided**. This is due to the **molecular structure** of ice, whose oxygen and hydrogen atoms are arranged in a hexagonal (six-sided) lattice.

● Oxygen
● Hydrogen

Snowflakes take many different forms, depending on variables such as temperature, but always with six sides.

Making glass

Glass is made by **melting a mixture** containing sand. When the liquid cools, it sets hard, but remains transparent. The molecules in glass are arranged irregularly, like those in a liquid. However, their strong bonds mean that glass is hard like a solid. This is called an **amorphous solid**. The regular crystals of sand are changed into an

irregular pattern.

Glass molecular structure

"This is not my best side!"

Bullet-proof

Glass is very hard, but its **irregular molecules** make it brittle, which means that it will break under only a small force. A bullet can easily break through glass without being slowed much at all. To make glass bulletproof, **layers of glass** are placed next to **layers of plastic**. The more layers there are, the stronger the glass becomes.

TRY THIS

Make your own crystal needles.

What you need:
A cup, Epsom salts (magnesium sulphate), hot tap water, food colouring (any colour)

In your cup, mix half a cup of Epsom salts with half a cup of hot tap water and a drop of food colouring. Stir thoroughly until all the salt has dissolved and place the cup in the refrigerator. After three hours, retrieve the cup and scoop out your crystals. The magnesium sulphate should have formed long, delicate needle crystals.

Hard as ice

When liquids are cooled, they freeze into solids. Most substances become smaller and denser when they freeze, but water expands when it freezes and ice floats on water.

10% of iceberg visible

"You all right down below?"

Hidden danger

About
90 per cent
of an iceberg is under water. Ice has a mass that is about 90 per cent the mass of
liquid water.
The mass of liquid water displaced by the underwater portion of the iceberg is equal to
the mass of the whole iceberg,
including the 10 per cent that is above the water level.

90% of iceberg not visible

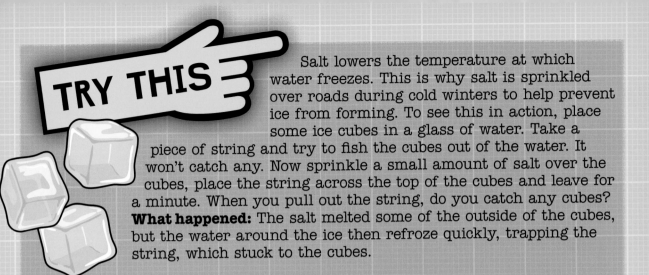

TRY THIS

Salt lowers the temperature at which water freezes. This is why salt is sprinkled over roads during cold winters to help prevent ice from forming. To see this in action, place some ice cubes in a glass of water. Take a piece of string and try to fish the cubes out of the water. It won't catch any. Now sprinkle a small amount of salt over the cubes, place the string across the top of the cubes and leave for a minute. When you pull out the string, do you catch any cubes? **What happened:** The salt melted some of the outside of the cubes, but the water around the ice then refroze quickly, trapping the string, which stuck to the cubes.

Slippery problem

Ice feels slippery to touch because it is covered in a thin layer of liquid water. Ice skates make the ice even more slippery by **melting some of the ice** as they pass over it. The skates melt the ice using a combination of **pressure and friction**. The ice refreezes after the skate has passed over it.

Water freezes into ice at a temperature of **0°C**. The ice remains slippery as it gets **colder** until it reaches a temperature of **-30°C**. At this temperature, ice is no longer covered in a layer of liquid water and is no longer slippery.

"No, it's a bit cold"

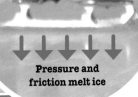

Pressure and friction melt ice

11

Boiling point

As they are heated, liquids turn into gas. The temperature at which they do this is called their boiling point. At sea-level atmospheric pressure, the boiling point of water is 100°C.

Under pressure

The higher **the pressure of the air** around it, **the higher** water's boiling point becomes. In a pressure cooker, the boiling point can go up as high as

130°C.

This cooks food much more quickly.

"Whoa, she's gonna blow."

At the top of high mountains, air pressure is reduced. At the summit of Mount Everest, water boils at a temperature of

70°C,

making it impossible to brew a cup of tea.

Snowing in space

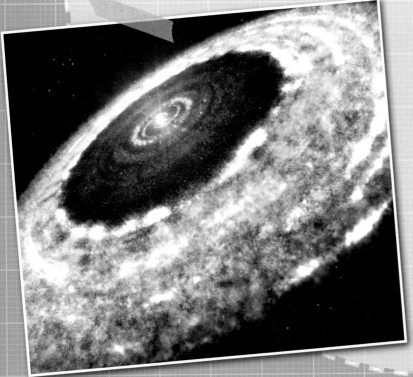

If lower pressure **decreases** water's boiling point, what happens to water in space, where there is almost **no pressure** but the temperature is **-270°C**? The answer is that it boils almost immediately, but then freezes again to form

snow crystals.

Disks of snow have been discovered surrounding young stars in distant galaxies.

Dry ice

Some solids pass straight from a solid form to a **gaseous form** without ever becoming a liquid. This is called **sublimation**. Carbon dioxide sublimates, and is used to create special effects on stage. Solid carbon dioxide is known as **dry ice**.

TRY THIS

Even at room temperature, liquid water changes into the gas water vapour in a process called evaporation. To see this at work, wet two identical pieces of cloth and wring out the excess water. Place one cloth in an airtight plastic bag and the other on an open tray and place them next to a window. Leave the cloths overnight. When you return, only the exposed cloth will have dried. The water molecules on the exposed cloth evaporated into the air, but those on the sealed cloth could not escape.

Mix it up

A solution is a mixture in which one substance is dissolved into another. The substance being dissolved is called the solute, while the substance that dissolves is called the solvent.

In a solution, the molecules of the solute are evenly spread among the molecules of the solvent.

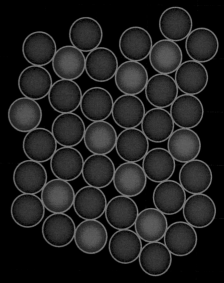

Solute molecules ○   Solvent molecules ●

Universal solvent

Water is known as the **'universal solvent'** as it is able to dissolve lots of other chemicals, such as salt. The water that comes out of your tap has various minerals dissolved in it. Some of the minerals separate out of the water when you boil it, and may leave a residue called

limescale

at the bottom of the kettle.

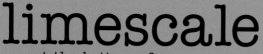

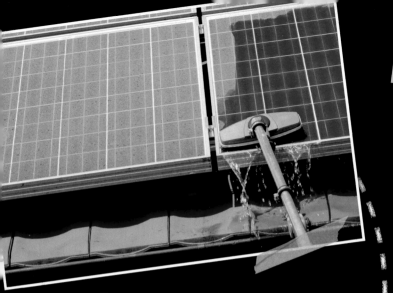

Pure water

Our saliva is salty, and we find water that matches the saltiness of our saliva the best to drink. If we were to drink pure water all the time, it would dissolve the minerals in our saliva and make us ill. Pure water can dissolve tiny specks of dirt, and is used to clean sensitive objects such as solar panels.

TRY THIS

What you'll need:
Four small plastic containers, water, salt, sand, oil, food colouring

Mix the water thoroughly in four separate containers each with one of the following: oil, sand, salt and food colouring. Shake and leave to settle. When the mixtures settle, which ones separate out and which have formed a solution?

Solid solution

Solutions can be **solid, liquid or gas**. Steel is an example of a solid solution, known as an alloy, made from iron mixed with carbon and other materials. Steel is

harder and
stronger

than pure iron.

"If it's that strong it'll hold my weight easily!"

Burn it!

Burning, or combustion, is a violent chemical reaction that produces lots of heat. A fire needs fuel and the gas oxygen, which is found in the air. Normally, heat is needed to get the chemical reaction started.

The flames from an explosion reach about

1,000°C.

Homo erectus made fires by rubbing sticks together to produce enough heat to start the burning.

"Erm, it might be too hot for those."

Controlling fire

Humans are the only animals that have discovered how to start and control fires. Fire provided our ancestors with a source of warmth and protection, and also allowed them to cook their food. *Homo erectus*, an ancestor of modern humans that lived

600,000 years ago,

is the earliest human known to have used fire in this way.

Fire air

Oxygen was discovered in 1781 by the Swedish chemist **Carl Wilhelm Scheele**, who called the gas 'fire air' due to the way substances burned in it. Before the discovery of oxygen, it was believed that burning materials contained a substance called

phlogiston,

which escaped into the air during burning.

Putting out fires

Fires can be stopped in three different ways:

Removing the oxygen

Without oxygen, a fire goes out immediately. Carbon dioxide fire extinguishers drive off the air and replace it with carbon dioxide.

Removing the heat

Pouring water on a fire cools it down. The water is heated to become steam, which escapes into the air, carrying away heat. But water can make some kinds of fire worse, and it should never be poured on burning fat.

Removing the fuel

Firebreaks stop the spread of forest fires by providing a gap with no flammable materials, which fires cannot cross.

Chemistry in the kitchen

Cooking is a way to break down the chemicals in our food and make them easier to digest. In fact, we are starting the digestion process before the food even enters our mouths! We need to cook our food – if we only ate completely raw food, we would quickly become ill.

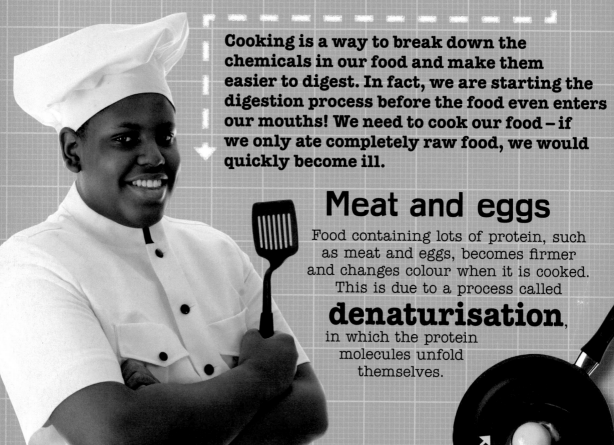

Meat and eggs

Food containing lots of protein, such as meat and eggs, becomes firmer and changes colour when it is cooked. This is due to a process called

denaturisation,

in which the protein molecules unfold themselves.

Uncooked egg

Vegetables

The cell walls of plants are made of a tough substance called cellulose. Cooking softens vegetables by breaking the cell walls so that they become soluble. This makes the vegetables easier to digest.

Tasty toast

When bread is toasted, the amino acids and sugars in the bread combine to form more complex chemicals. One of these chemicals, acetyl tetrahydropyridine, gives toast its distinctive taste. Cook the bread too long, and the complex chemicals break down into chunks of carbon – burnt toast.

Scientific cooking

Many modern chefs use science to create new flavours to surprise diners. **Spherification** is the creation of balls of liquid food surrounded by a gel membrane. The membrane is created using a substance found in algae.

These spheres look like fish eggs, but they in fact contain liquefied raspberries.

British chef Heston Blumenthal has created an ice cream that tastes of bacon and egg. He makes it by adding bacon to scrambled egg and using liquid nitrogen to flash-freeze the mixture and lock in the flavours.

Fried egg

TRY THIS

To make a meringue, you need three egg whites and 150 g of caster sugar. Place the egg whites in a bowl and use a whisk to beat them until they become stiff. Add one tablespoon of sugar to the mixture and whisk it until it becomes stiff again. Repeat this process until all the sugar has been added. The mixture should be thick and glossy. Scoop 16 small balls of mixture onto a piece of baking paper and bake for an hour at 140°C.

What happened when you whisked the egg?
Beating the egg white with the whisk unfolded the protein molecules.

High-energy matter

In addition to solids, liquids and gases, there is a fourth state of matter known as plasma. Plasma is similar to a gas, but negatively charged electrons have broken off the atoms, leaving positively charged ions. Turning a gas into a plasma requires lots of energy.

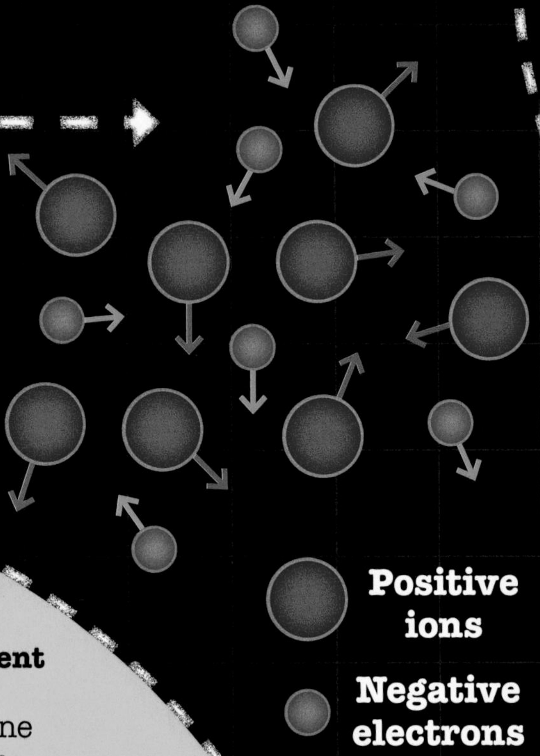

Positive ions

Negative electrons

Glowing plasma

Neon lights work by passing an **electric current** through the gas **neon** and turning it into **plasma**. The charged particles collide with one another, giving off a red glow. Neon plasma always gives off red light. Using a mixture of other gases, it is possible to make more than

150
different colours.

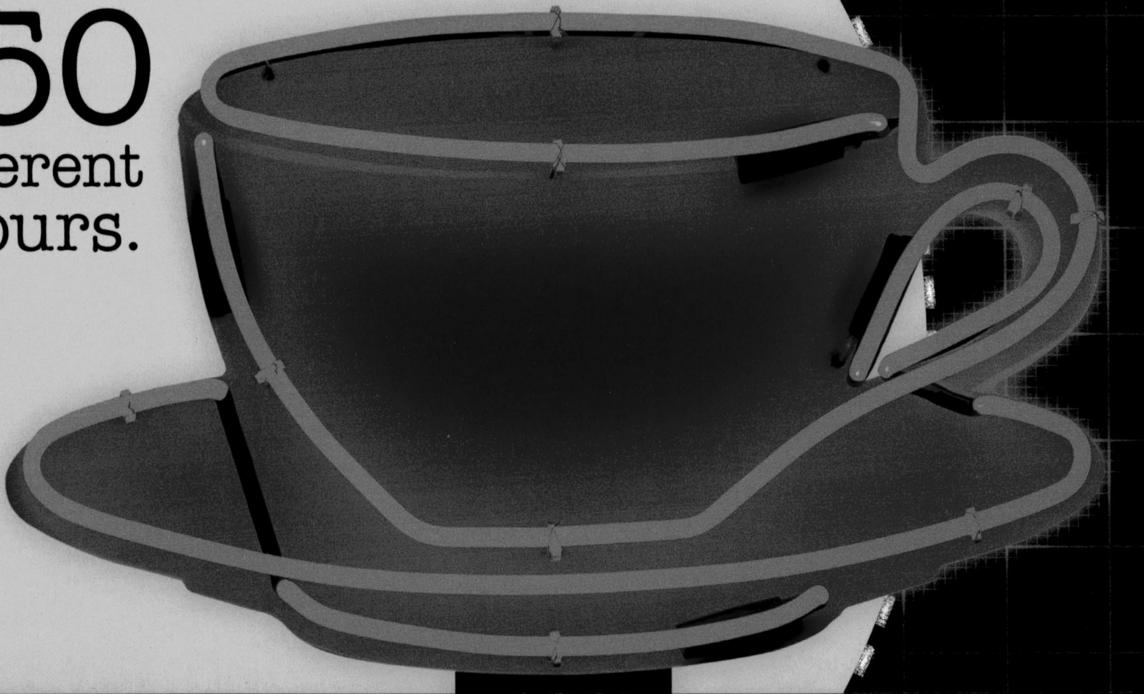

Hot balls of plasma

It is thought that **99 per cent** of all the visible matter in the Universe is in the form of plasma. The Sun and other stars are hot balls made mostly of plasma.

Night lights

The Northern and Southern Lights are a spectacular display of light in the night sky that are seen near the Poles. They are produced when **high-energy plasma** particles from the Sun interact with gas molecules high in the atmosphere. Near the equator, Earth's magnetic field deflects the particles, but the field is weaker near the poles, and enough plasma gets through to produce this spectacular light show.

This pale-green glow above Iceland has been produced by reactions between plasma from the Sun and oxygen molecules about 100 kilometres above the surface of Earth.

Moulding shapes

We are surrounded by objects that have been moulded into shape then set hard to become solid. These new shapes allow us to create all kinds of useful tools.

Pottery

Humans have been making pots from clay for more than 20,000 years. Clay is a **special kind of earth** that, when mixed with water, is **extremely flexible** and can be made into all kinds of shapes. After it has been moulded into the desired shape, it is baked in a **super-hot kiln** at temperatures of over 1,000°C. This makes it rock-hard and **water resistant**, which means that clay pots are perfect as storage containers.

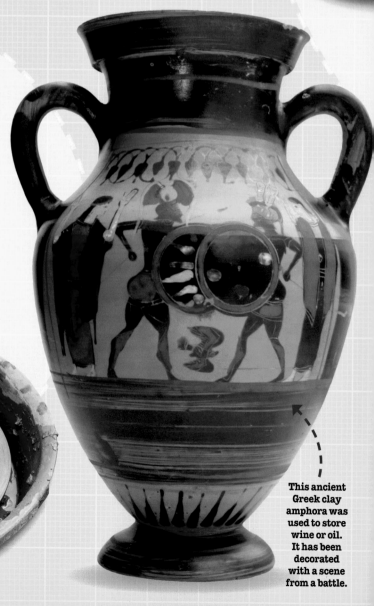

This ancient Greek clay amphora was used to store wine or oil. It has been decorated with a scene from a battle.

Plastics

Today, most of the moulded objects we use are made from plastic, a synthetic material extracted from petroleum. Different plastics may be soft or hard, depending on how they were made. All these objects are made from a form of plastic.

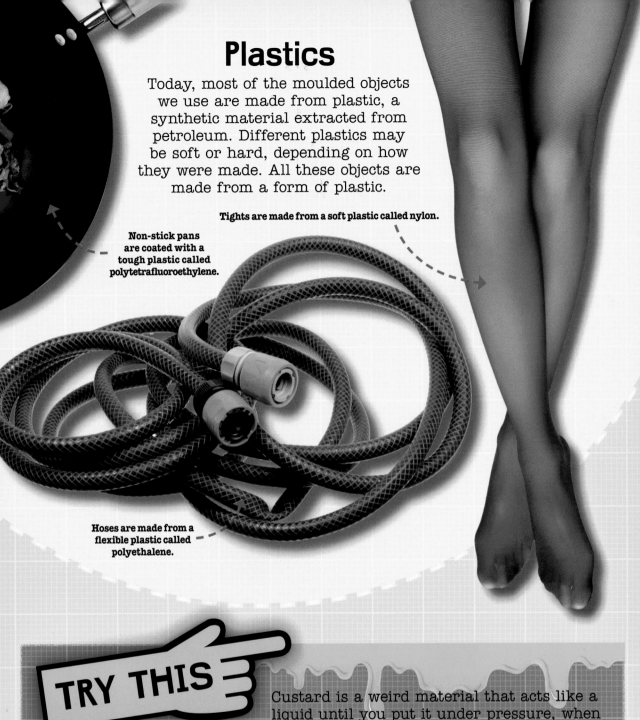

Tights are made from a soft plastic called nylon.

Non-stick pans are coated with a tough plastic called polytetrafluoroethylene.

Hoses are made from a flexible plastic called polyethalene.

TRY THIS

Custard is a weird material that acts like a liquid until you put it under pressure, when it suddenly starts acting like a solid. See this by making a bowl of custard. Mix the custard powder with water until it feels strange to do so. That means it's properly mixed. Now take some of the custard and roll it into a ball with your hands. If you keep rolling the custard around, it feels solid, but see what happens when you stop!

What happened?
Custard contains tiny grains of corn flour. Put those grains under pressure and they hold together like a solid. Let go, and they fall around one another like a liquid.

Super-strong materials

Carbon fibre

Graphite is a soft solid that is easily broken, but thin filaments of graphite woven together are **very strong**. They are added to plastics to make a strong but lightweight material called **carbon fibre**. Formula 1 racing was revolutionised by carbon fibre. In 1981, McLaren made the first car with a carbon-fibre chassis. Its light weight made the car fast, but its strength has also saved lives when cars have crashed.

The 1981 McLaren (above) had a carbon-fibre body. In modern F1 cars such as the 2014 Mercedes (below), the suspension and wings are also made from carbon fibre.

Hair

Carbon fibre

Each of the fibres in carbon fibre is just a few **millionths** of a metre in diameter. That's thinner than a human hair.

Kevlar®

Kevlar® is a **super-strong plastic**. It has a very high tensile strength, meaning that it is hard to pull apart, and is used to make body armour, such as protective vests for police officers.

POLICE

Copying nature

Spider silk is a **super-strong**, super-light material made by spiders to **build their webs**, to catch prey or to hang on to. Scientists study spider silk to see what makes it so strong. In 2015, a company claimed to have started making artificial silk by copying a spider's spinneret. This light but strong material would be perfect for manufacturing machines such as aeroplanes, and one day many objects around us may be made of silk.

A spider produces silk using an organ called a spinneret, located on the underside of its abdomen.

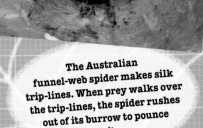

The Australian funnel-web spider makes silk trip-lines. When prey walks over the trip-lines, the spider rushes out of its burrow to pounce on it.

Smart materials

Smart materials are materials that are changed by variations in conditions such as temperature, light or pressure. This change is reversible and can be repeated many times.

Shape-memory alloys

Spectacle frames can be made from shape-memory alloys (SMAs). If you sit on the frames and bend them, you can just put them in some **hot water** and they'll return to their original shape.

Memory foam

Many modern mattresses are made from a material called memory foam, which has the property of being **'visco-elastic'**. The 'visco' part means that it changes shape slowly when pressure is applied, while 'elastic' means it returns to its original shape when pressure is removed, but it only does so slowly. This means that the mattress moulds itself to your body shape, making for a super-comfortable sleep.

Now used to line matresses, memory foam was originally developed by NASA in the 1960s to make aircraft cushions.

Pressure pads

Piezoelectric materials produce an

electric current

when they're squeezed. They are used in alarm
systems – when somebody treads on them,
they start an electric current and
set off the alarm.

Moon

Sun

Sensitive to the sun

These materials change colour when exposed to different
amounts of light. Photochromic sunglasses get

darker in bright sunlight,

then lighten up again when you go inside. They react to the
invisible ultraviolet light that is produced by the Sun.

Quiz

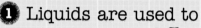

1 Liquids are used to **move the arms** of this digger. This works because:
a) liquids **can be** easily **compressed**
b) liquids **cannot be** easily **compressed**
c) liquids have a **fixed shape**

2 Which of these arrangements **of carbon atoms** is **diamond**, and which is **graphite**?

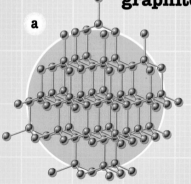

a   b

3 If **100 cubic metres** of an iceberg is visible above the surface of the ocean, what is the **volume** of the whole iceberg?

4 Water **boils** at a **lower temperature** at the top of **high mountains** than at sea level because:
a) it is **much colder** at the **top** of mountains
b) **the force of gravity** is **reduced** at the top of mountains
c) **air pressure** is **reduced** at the top of mountains

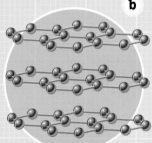

"Anyone for tea?"

5 Which of these molecular structures is **not that** of a crystal?

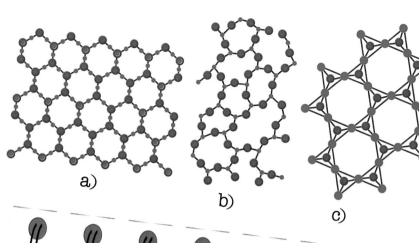

a)

b)

c)

6 For fires to burn, **which gas** needs to be present?

7 An egg white **changes colour** when it is cooked because:
a) the **protein molecules** unfold themselves
b) the **cellulose** is broken down
c) the **sugars combine** into more complex chemicals

8 **Steel** is an **alloy of iron** mixed with which **other material**?

29

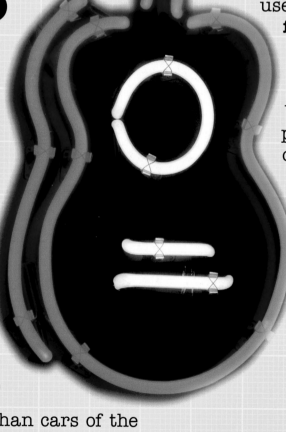

9 What is the name for the **state of matter** of the

neon

in this glowing sign?
a) gas
b) liquid
c) solid
d) plasma

10 Carbon dioxide gas changes directly from

a solid to a

gas

without passing through a liquid stage. **What is the name for this process?**

11 **Racing cars** whose bodies are made of **carbon fibre** can **go faster** than cars of the same strength whose bodies are made of metal. **Why is this?**

12 # Tensile strength

is a measure of what?
a) How easily a material **will bend**
b) How easily a material can be **pulled apart**
c) How easily a material can be **scratched**

13 Which is the smart

material

used to make the **frames** for some glasses?
a) Shape- memory alloy
b) Photochromic plastic
c) Memory foam

Glossary

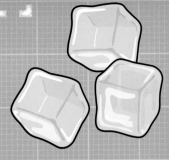

Amorphous solid
A solid, such as glass, whose molecules are arranged in an irregular pattern.

Atom
The smallest particle of a substance that can exist by itself.

Chemical reaction
A process during which two or more substances interact with one another to produce new substances.

Clay
A thick, heavy soil that is soft when it is wet. Clay can be moulded into pots that become hard and waterproof when they are fired.

Crystal
A solid whose atoms or molecules are arranged in a regular pattern.

Elasticity
A property of a solid that returns to its original shape after it has been stretched or squashed.

Evaporate
To change state from a liquid to a gas.

Gas
A state of matter in which the atoms or molecules are not bonded to one another but move randomly in all directions.

Hydraulics
A system in which forces are transmitted using liquids.

Liquid
A state of matter in which the atoms or molecules are bonded but can move past one another. A liquid has no fixed shape and can flow from one place to another.

Molecule
A tiny particle of matter made from two or more atoms that are bonded together.

Plasma
A highly energetic state of matter similar to a gas, in which the atoms have broken apart.

Plastic
A synthetic material that can be moulded into any shape when hot. It sets hard in that shape when it cools.

Solid
A state of matter in which the atoms or molecules are strongly bonded to one another and fixed in place.

Solution
A mixture in which one substance, called the solute, is dissolved evenly in another substance, called the solvent. A solution may be a solid, liquid or gas.

Spinneret
The organ on a spider's abdomen that produces silk.

Tensile strength
A measure of how hard it is to pull a material apart.

Index

Answers

1. b)
2. a) is diamond b) is graphite
3. The iceberg is 1,000 cubic metres in volume. 10 per cent is visible, which means that the whole iceberg is 10 times larger than the visible part.
4. c)
5. b) is not a crystal. This is not a regular lattice structure.
6. Oxygen
7. a)
8. Carbon
9. d)
10. Sublimation
11. Carbon-fibre cars are lighter than metal cars of the same strength.
12. b)
13. a)

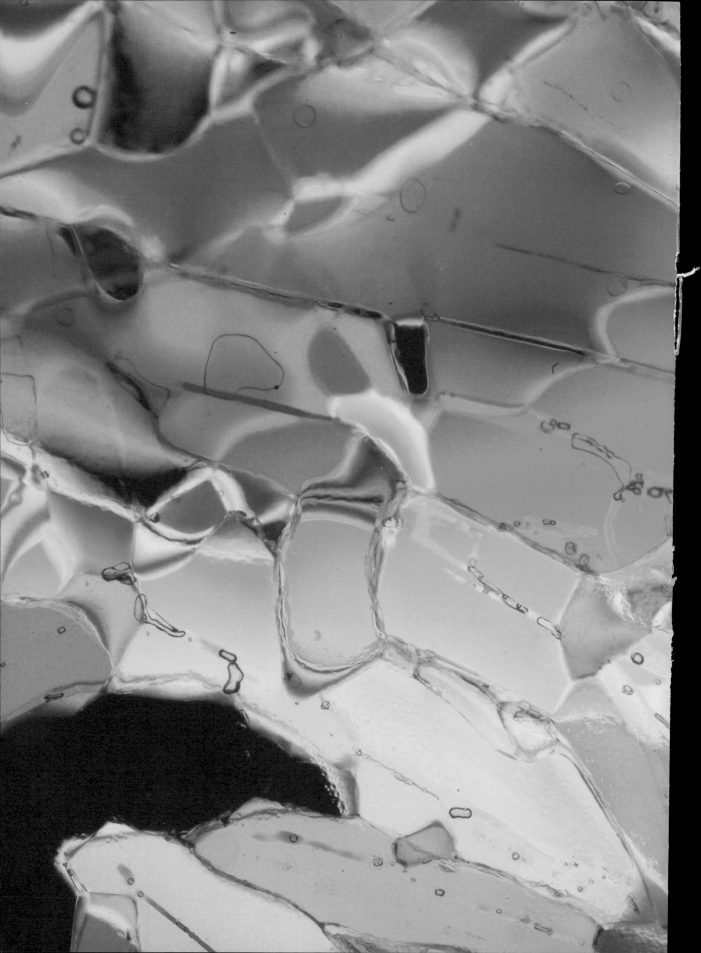